LOVE YOUR NEIGHBOR

Restoring Dignity,
Breaking the Cycle of Poverty

Kathryn Feliciano

INSTITUTE FOR
FAITH, WORK
& ECONOMICS

First Edition, 2016

ISBN 978-0-9975369-3-5

Published by the

Institute for Faith, Work & Economics

8400 Westpark Drive

Suite 100

McLean, Virginia 22102

www.tifwe.org

LOVE YOUR NEIGHBOR

Restoring Dignity,
Breaking the Cycle of Poverty

CONTENTS

INTRODUCTION

Americans gave $358.38 billion in charity in 2014.[1] They also volunteered 7.9 billion hours, valued at approximately $175 billion.[2] Billions more dollars were contributed to fight poverty through Medicare, Medicaid, welfare, food stamps and other federal poverty relief programs that year. Yet, the poverty rate in the United States went unchanged. In both 2013 and 2014, it was 14.8 percent.[3] There were still over 46 million people living in poverty in the United States in 2014.[4] Our charity, our time, our taxpayer dollars did not have a measurable effect on the poor.

The traditional method of charity is not working to lift the poor out of poverty. Traditional charity can be defined as handouts to the poor. It is giving someone a bowl of soup or clothes to wear. It is a welfare check, putting a few dollars in the homeless man's cup, or planting flowers in the seedy side of town. Charity is a short-term solution to a long-term problem. When provided in the context of catastrophe, charity and aid are essential. However, charity in the context of development, even though given out of compassion and good intentions, does not create positive change, as we see in the statistics above. Charity is provision for the poor; it does not incentivize the poor to provide for themselves. Charity gives a person a plate of food; it does not equip them to to get their own food in the future. Charity is done outside of relationship with the poor; it does not know who it is helping and does not have the flexibility to care for each individual in the ways they need.

By donating to charities and even volunteering at such charities, in the context of development, we often end up hurting the very people we are trying to help. Unintentionally, we often take away the dignity of the poor, act superior to them, and create entitlement by providing them with an easy short-term solution. We put a Band-Aid on the problem, but do not create lasting change. In *Toxic Charity*, Robert D. Lupton writes, "When we do for those in need what they have the capacity to do for themselves, we disempower them…Giving to those in need what they could be gaining from their own initiative may well be the kindest way to destroy people."[5]

It is time to reevaluate how we "help" people. This call to change the way we serve the poor has become prevalent in poverty relief literature. Books such as *For the Least of These: A Biblical Answer to Poverty, When Helping Hurts,* and *Toxic Charity,* and movies like *Poverty, Inc.* show that not all poverty alleviation programs are helpful. The common theme in this body of work is that fighting poverty is not easy. Compassion alone will not get us the results we desire. We must be aware of the unintended consequences caused by traditional charity. Our good intentions can end up doing more damage than good for the people we are trying to serve.

From this literature, it is clear that often our poverty-fighting efforts do not work. We want to be more effective and more helpful. But how? We've all been there—we've seen people struggling to make ends meet, homeless people on the side of the road, hungry children; the list goes on. Our hearts are filled with compassion at the sight. We want to help people, but what is the best way to do this?

When I was growing up I heard of great need and wanted to help. I remember wobbling back and forth across a university campus lawn, trying to balance a bucket of water on my head. I was at a missions-based summer camp, and we were learning about the lack of clean water in Malawi. As the bucket of water began to topple off my head, the camp counselors explained the plight of Malawian women. These women walk miles to access clean water and bring it back to their families. They often carry this water on their heads to keep their hands free during this difficult trek.

This inspired me. I didn't know how to help, but I wanted to do something. I went home and threw a huge fundraiser at my church for an organization that drilled wells in Africa. The event was a success in my eyes, with a swarm of students coming to an indoor carnival and making donations as part of their entrance fee. We showed a video about drilling wells in Malawi, called for more donations, and everyone had a great time. With thousands of dollars raised, we all felt like we had made a difference.

After we sent the money to the organization, I never found out what they did with the donations. Did a well get drilled? Did people have access to clean water in their community? Did we really help anyone?

These questions might be familiar to you if you've been involved in the fight against poverty. If you haven't, they certainly will come up. Many of us are inspired to serve the poor in our community and abroad, but we don't really know how to do that. We are compelled by compassion, but are often unsure if we are helping at all. We donate to charities and volunteer for organizations devoted to alleviating poverty, but is our time and money actually helping or hurting the poor?

If you are wrestling with these issues and asking, "how can I effectively serve the poor?", this booklet is for you. It will help you utilize your local knowledge and creativity to make a difference in your community. This booklet will not answer all your questions about poverty. It will not provide a one-size-fits-all solution or lay out a theoretical framework that helps nations transform from developing to developed. It won't debate how to eliminate corruption or fix public education systems. It *will* help you think through the needs of your community, how your gifts and talents can be used to fight poverty, and what kinds of organizations you should support. It will help you serve the poor in your community in an effective and sustainable way. It is biblically based, informed by economics, and focused on application.

The first half of the booklet will lay out biblical truths foundational to a principled approach to poverty-fighting programs. The second half of the booklet consists of stories and a group exercise that will empower you to best serve the poor in your community. The group exercise will take dedication and commitment. Poverty is vast, multi-faceted, and complicated. Finding ways to come alongside the poor in their fight to flourish will be similarly difficult. This booklet can foster great conversation. Consider reading through it with a friend or a small group that can be a sounding board.

Why is this booklet so focused on the practical applications of how to serve the poor in your community? First, poverty is an immense issue. It stretches across the globe, swallowing up people, communities, and countries. It affects all ages, races, religions, and cultures. You simply cannot tackle all the aspects of poverty in one booklet. Second, by God's grace, there are already solid, biblically-based resources that discuss the theoretical aspects of poverty. Those mentioned above and many more are listed in the Bibliography. This booklet will draw from and strive to extend the literature by discussing how you and I can practically live out our Christian call to serve the least of these.

CHAPTER 1: **THE CALL TO SERVE THE POOR**

Who Are the Poor?

There are several types of poverty—material, social, psychological, and spiritual. There is poverty internationally and domestically (that is, poverty outside of and inside of your country). For the purposes of this book, the word "poor," will refer to the materially poor, though throughout the booklet we will find it is essential to address all aspects of poverty. We will discuss some ways to help the global poor, but much of our discussion will focus on the poor who live in your community.

In this booklet, we will generally define poverty as a lack of means to make choices that meet a variety of critical needs. To put it more simply, poverty is a lack of options.

Sure, the material poor do not have enough money. Some don't have shelter, and many don't have food. These are aspects of poverty. But poverty is far more than that. The materially poor are limited in their resources, and therefore have much fewer options available to them. Take the following choices. These are things we take for granted but may not be available to the poor.

- When can I spend time with family and friends this week?
- Which college should I attend?
- Should I buy kale at Trader Joe's, or spinach?
- What neighborhood should I live in?

Many of us wouldn't think twice about this list. But, consider Victoria. She is a widow with a high school education and two kids. She works two jobs to make enough money to care for her kids and afford her rent in southeast Washington, DC. She works upwards of sixty hours a week, leaving little time for her to spend with her family, much less her friends. Her income from two part-time jobs can't pay for college for her children. She can provide her children with food, but sacrifices nutritional value so they can stay on budget. With rent costs soaring in DC, they settled in a neighborhood that isn't violent, but it certainly is not crime-free. Her kids go to the local public school. The school has had some trouble with gang violence, but it's not a constant threat. Still, her kids don't seem to be challenged or thriving. She rarely sees them doing homework or studying, and they have been getting into some trouble lately. What can she do?

Victoria doesn't have a lot of good options to promote flourishing in her family. She and her family are stuck in this situation. She could try going back to school to find better employment. But how? She can barely afford rent and food for her children. Victoria grew up in a poor family. She wants her kids to have a shot at a life she didn't have, but she can't afford to move into a different neighborhood to get them out of their current public school. She doesn't have the means to make a choice that will change their situation.

Or how about Chris, an ex-gang member in Los Angeles? He served his time. He experienced the consequences of being in a gang, and he wants to start over. But all his friends are gang members. His family isn't around. No one will hire him. He has a record and doesn't have a high school education. Without employment, he can't rent an apartment. He has no job, no apartment, no friends. What can he do? The most reasonable choice would be to rejoin the gang. They'll take care of him like a family. He can sell drugs and make money. He'll be able to afford an apartment and food.

This definition also applies to the international poor, and shows there are even worse tradeoffs in the developing world. Imagine a Malawian mother named Melina. She needs to provide her children and husband with water, but the closest well is several miles away. She has no choice but to walk to the well each day, performing backbreaking labor to provide her family with clean water while her husband works on a small farm. The many hours she spends on this task prevents her from making other choices that will help her family out of poverty, such as doubling their small garden plot or even starting a microbusiness. Until Melina can find another way to get clean water, her options are limited.

Poverty is a lack of options. Steve Corbett and Brian Fikkert, authors of *When Helping Hurts,* affirm this definition of poverty, saying, "According to Nobel Laureate Amartya Sen, it is this lack of freedom to be able to make meaningful choices—to have an ability to affect one's situation—that is the distinguishing feature of poverty."[6]

Now, you may say, Chris was in a gang. He had a choice, and made the wrong one. He must suffer the consequences. While there's truth to that, there's also truth to the idea that he has paid the price established by society for his wrong choice. And furthermore, there's truth in the gospel—that as we have been afforded grace and mercy by God, we're to extend grace and mercy toward each other.

The Christian Call to Serve the Poor

If someone is materially poor and they want to make choices that help them rise out of poverty, we are called to help them, regardless of whether their poverty is the result of past choices (like Chris) or not (like Melina), or even a blend of both (perhaps like Victoria). It is a crucial piece of the Christian faith. There are thousands of verses in the Bible about our response and responsibility to the poor (see Mark 12:30 31; 1 John 3:17 18; Prov. 14:31; Isa. 1:17; James 2:13, 15 17; Zech. 7:8 10; Matt. 25:34036, 40).[7] They remind us of our call to love our neighbors as ourselves and serve the least of these with mercy and justice. In these passages, we read that we should be just, plead the widow's call, not oppress the fatherless, give food to the hungry, and clothe those who are naked. We need to understand how these passages fit together with one another and with God's grand storyline of the Bible. Based on these and other passages about the poor, what is the overall goal in fighting poverty? How should we go about doing it?

The Goal

Human flourishing is a key biblical theme woven throughout the whole Bible. Jonathan Pennington, professor at Southern Seminary, defines biblical flourishing as "being in a right wholeness relationship with God."[8] The vision of biblical flourishing is eternal and abundant life in the presence of God. The means is trusting in Jesus Christ for salvation, which restores our original relationship with God. However, biblical flourishing is not limited to the spiritual aspects of our relationship with God; it encompasses all our being, including our material, psychological, and emotional aspects.

Understanding flourishing enhances how we view God's redemption for Christians in Christ. God is working throughout the Old and New Testament to redeem his broken people. He is actively carrying out his grand plan to have his people in his place under his rule for his glory and our good.[9] When we consider this great truth, we tend to separate our relationship with God from all other things. But, God is redeeming his people not in part, but in whole. Pennington writes,

> All this means that at its core and in its very essence, God's saving work, his redemptive activity, his goal for humanity and all creation is precisely this: that we flourish fully even as he himself flourishes perfectly, completely, and with overflowing abundance... We should cease thinking of spirituality and godliness as something that has nothing to do with human well-being and flourishing, including in a physical, economic, psychological, and relational sense.[10]

If God desires flourishing for us in a "physical, economic, psychological, and relational sense," then as Christians we should fight poverty in this way.[11] To be clear, aiming for biblical flourishing does not mean that we all will have perfect lives. Jesus does not promise Christians an easy life. But aiming for flourishing does mean our poverty alleviation goal goes beyond helping the poor materially. Flourishing looks like hope in Christ, dignity in knowing that we were made in the image of God, the fulfillment that comes from work and taking care of your family, and joy in meaningful relationships, especially with our Creator. Biblical flourishing will always be incomplete in this world, for full flourishing will only be realized with the second coming of Christ. However incomplete our efforts, our goal for fighting poverty should be in line with this vision.

The Means

If biblical flourishing is our goal, we must serve the whole person. To do this, we must *truly* love our neighbors. In Romans 13:8-10, we read the following:

> Owe no one anything, except to love each other, for the one who loves another has fulfilled the law. For the commandments, "You shall not commit adultery, You shall not murder, You shall not steal, You shall not covet," and any other commandment, are summed up in this word: "You shall love your neighbor as yourself." Love does no wrong to a neighbor; therefore love is the fulfilling of the law.

Paul compels us to love God by loving one another, in order that we fulfill the Law. He ends by stating, "Love does no wrong to a neighbor." He is talking about loving our neighbors by fulfilling the law—by not committing adultery, stealing, or coveting our neighbors, for example. We can apply this same concept to poverty. Our efforts to fight against poverty and for flourishing are spurred on by our love for our neighbor. In serving the poor, we need to make sure our love is not doing harm in the process. Otherwise it isn't love.

To love the poor well, we have two responsibilities—preach the gospel to them and help them out of poverty. Fighting poverty without sharing the gospel does not allow the poor to fully flourish, for you cannot fully flourish without knowing Christ. On the other hand, we cannot simply tell the poor about Christ and not help them with their situation. As James writes, "If a brother or sister is without clothing and in need of daily food, and one of you says to them, 'Go in peace, be warmed and be filled,' and yet you do not give them what is necessary for their body, what use is that? Even so faith, if it has no works, is dead, being by itself" (James 2:15-17). We have a real call to serve the poor, not just in word but also in deed. As we do this, we must be helpful in the long term. We must remember that providing the poor with material goods, as with charity, is a caring act that will help the poor for a short time. But, it does not enact long-term change; the methods we use to serve the poor must target more than just the current situation. Coupled with the saving grace of Jesus Christ, which causes dramatic change in people's lives, poverty efforts will be far more effective.

Who Can We Help?

We see the clear calls of Scripture to help the poor, but the sheer enormity and complicated nature of poverty can be intimidating. Burnout and cynicism are the constant companions of many engaged in this work, but they aren't impossible to counter. By recognizing our limits, we can take better advantage of our finite capacities to maximize our personal contributions, and continue to glorify Christ in our endurance and obedience.

Pennington sums this up in his paper "Sell All Your Possessions":

> The Scriptures, both Old and New Testaments, speak much about the importance of care for the poor and those in need...Christians are called to employ whatever goods they have for the good of others. The practical outworking is a matter of wisdom, not a matter of rules and regulations. God loves a cheerful giver (2 Cor. 9:7) and Christians are under no compulsion to meet every need that presents itself. Even giving up all of one's wealth and possessions would not meet all the needs of the world! But Christians are under obligation to be motivated by a heart of love and compassion for others. This fulfills the second greatest commandment, that we love one another.[12]

Pennington reiterates the call for Christians to serve the poor laid out in both the Old and New Testaments. He also helps us understand that we cannot fix poverty on our own. As Christians, we should have an attitude of compassion and mercy and a heart for serving others. While our job as individual Christians is to serve the poor, our goal should not be to eradicate poverty for every person, for that goal is impossible. We must do our part, work with our brothers and sisters in Christ, and rely on and take comfort in the Lord's sovereignty.

We have presented three ideas in this section:

1. Poverty is a lack of suitable options.
2. As Christians, we are called to serve the poor.
3. As finite individuals, we are limited.

Next, we will look at biblical truths and principles that will help us tackle these problems in a holistic, effective way.

CHAPTER 2: **BIBLICAL TRUTHS & PRINCIPLES FOR FLOURISHING**

The world is ravaged by poverty and the way we strive to fight poverty isn't working. Our goal is flourishing, and the means to achieve this goal is true gospel-centered love for the poor. We need principles to help us know how to help the poor out of poverty, and that is the goal of this section. I will provide three principles, which are biblically-informed rules of thumb for fighting poverty and pursuing flourishing. Each principle is based on a biblical truth. The goal of this list is not to be comprehensive. Rather, the goal is to give you three criteria so that when you are presented with an opportunity to fight poverty, you can assess if it is an effective way to serve the poor.

As Image Bearers, We Should Respect One Another

Let's start with the first biblical truth and principle for flourishing:

> *Biblical Truth 1:* We are created in God's image.
> *Flourishing Principle 1.* Respect the dignity and gifts of each human being.

Where does this biblical truth come from? We see it in the very beginning of creation. Genesis 1:27 says, "So God created man in his own image, in the image of God he created him; male and female he created them." God created mankind, both men and women, in his image. No other living, breathing thing on this earth has the honor of reflecting the image of God in this way. Right away, we realize this fact is significant. We get to image God. What does this mean?

In an article called, "Man—Made in the Image of God," Don Dunavant writes,

> Three authors provide helpful theological direction for us. Wayne Grudem pointed out that the words used in Genesis 1:26-27, "image" (*tselem*) and "likeness" (*demut*) in the Hebrew "refer to something that is similar but not identical to the thing that it represents or is the 'image'

of." Therefore, Genesis 1:26, "would have meant to the original readers, 'Let us make man to be *like* us and to *represent* us." Bruce Ware noted that "the image of God in man involves God's creation of divine representations (images of God) who, in relationship with God and each other, function to represent God (imaging God) in carrying out God's designated responsibilities." Anthony Hoekema wrote that the image of God "describes not just something that man *has*, but something that man *is*" (emphasis his).[13]

As image bearers of Christ, we *are* something different. We are called to represent God, to be like Jesus, to live in relationship with God and one another, and to live life in such a way that we carry out the responsibilities the Lord has given us. We are made in God's image and have the honor and obligation of reflecting God's glory. We are "a crown of beauty in the hand of the Lord, a royal diadem in the hand of your God" (Isa. 62:3). Our main purpose is to live a life that reflects God's image and character in all that he has called us to do, for his glory.

In Glenn Sunshine's article, "The Image of God and Human Dignity," he shows us that being made in the image of God gives us responsibility and dignity. He writes, "the value of human life flows from the image of God, (and therefore) so does human dignity. And since the image of God is shared by all people, all of us have **an intrinsic dignity** that is distinct from anything else about us" (emphasis his).[14] Being made in the image of God teaches us that we have value and dignity, and we should respect everyone since they are also image bearers.

What about after the Fall? Were our image-bearing capabilities destroyed? Genesis 9 provides some insight here. This passage comes after the Fall. In it, God blesses Noah and his family. He starts by telling them, as in Genesis 1:28, "to be fruitful and multiply and fill the earth." God then blesses Noah and his family, saying that he gives them every animal and plant. After listing all the types of animals and plants, God puts it more directly: "I give you everything." Then the passage switches gear. Verse 6 says, "Whoever sheds the blood of man, by man shall his blood be shed, for God made man in his own image." While Noah and his family have dominion over all the earth and have been given everything, there are strict consequences for causing the death of another human being. Verse 6 shows us the significance of humankind. Our blood matters. Why? Because God made us in his own image. The fact that we are made in the image of God gives us worth, even after the Fall.

In an article, "Reflected Glory," J.I. Packer shows us that our goal has remained the same, even though our image-bearing capability has been marred by the Fall. We are still able to and should image God, but we need Jesus who fully reflects God's image, and reconciles us with the Father. He writes,

> We still bear the image of God *formally*...and so the unique dignity of each human being must still be recognized and respected (Gen. 9:6; James 3:9), as a gesture of honor to our maker. But we have lost the image *substantially*, and it takes God's grace-gift of union with Christ to restore it fully. Through this gift we share his resurrection life in regeneration, sanctification, and glorification (emphasis his).[15]

Being made in the image of God gives us inherent dignity. As such, our goal is to give God glory. But we cannot image God perfectly. We need Jesus, who is "the radiance of God's glory and exact representation of his being" (Heb. 1:3) to truly achieve this goal.

As we fight poverty, we must consider that every single person is created in God's image.

Dignity is defined in the Oxford dictionary as "the state or quality of being worthy of honor or respect," or "a sense of pride in oneself, self-respect."[16] Poverty affects more than just material possessions. It affects the way the poor view themselves, which we will discuss more fully in another section. For now, let's consider what current poverty-fighting solutions communicate to the poor. Many fail to account for people's inherent dignity and their gifts and talents. These programs should communicate to the poor, "*You* are of value, let me come alongside you and help *you* use *your* gifts and talents to grow." Instead, programs that provide handouts say, "*I* am better than you. You are in trouble, let *me* use *my* gifts and talents to help you get out of this mess."

Think about Jesus as he came to serve the poor in spirit. He *is* our Savior. But that was not his attitude. He broke bread with tax collectors, prostitutes, and sinners. He was born in a manger, a carpenter's son. He washed the feet of his disciples, even the feet of Judas Iscariot who was already contemplating betraying him. Jesus was the epitome of humility. As it says in Philippians, Jesus "humbled himself by becoming obedient to the point of death, even death on a cross,"[17] to save his people and care for their spiritual poverty.

We must embrace this same attitude as we start our journey in caring for the poor in a biblical and effective way. We must act with humility. If we truly believe that all people are made in the image of God, treating those we serve with dignity and respect must be at the core of any poverty-fighting program.

We All Have Gifts to Use for God's Glory

Biblical Truth 2: We are made with unique and specific gifts and talents, and we are called to steward those gifts for God's glory.

Flourishing Principle 2: We should use our gifts and talents to come alongside the poor, empowering them to further use their gifts and talents to live out their callings to work, family, community, and church.

Flipping back to Genesis, read Genesis 1:28: "And God blessed them. And God said to them, 'Be fruitful and multiply and fill the earth and subdue it, and have dominion over the fish of the sea and over the birds of the heavens and over every living thing that moves on the earth.'"

This verse is called the cultural mandate. It is the charge God has given his people to live for his glory, having been made in his image. "Be fruitful and multiply and fill the earth" refers to evangelism, discipleship, and childbearing. It is a call to bring about fruitful relationships that glorify God and spread the truth of the gospel. "Subdue (the earth), and have dominion over (it)" calls us to create and innovate. This command compels us to work. It urges us to create cultures and civilizations for God's glory. The cultural mandate exhorts us to glorify God by sharing the gospel and participating in meaningful work.

In *All Things New*, Hugh Whelchel highlights that God has given us gifts and talents in order to faithfully fulfill the cultural mandate. He writes,

> God has blessed his people with resources, gifts, and talents. Our job on earth is to steward and manage those resources to his glory…God gives us these resources so that we can fulfill the cultural mandate… While we cannot perfectly maximize all our resources, we can still use them to the best of our ability in a way that honors God. This is good stewardship.[18]

Where do we see in the Bible that we have been given these gifts? In Romans 12:4-6, Paul writes, "For as in one body we have many members, and the members do not all have the same function, so we, though many, are one body in Christ, and individually members one of another. Having gifts that differ according to the grace given to us, let us use them." Paul shows us that we have been given gifts to use for God's glory and to fulfill our role in the body of Christ. These talents and abilities have been given to us to serve the Lord and our community. Our goal is to steward them well. We will see this also in 1 Corinthians 12:12-17 in the next section when we discuss the body of Christ. Each one of us has a role to play, and God has equipped us to fulfill that role.

How should we use these gifts and talents for God's glory? Whelchel writes,

> Our primary calling to please and glorify God should always lead to a number of secondary callings; our call to the Church, family, community, and vocation. We discern the difference between our primary calling 'to be' and our secondary callings 'to do' when we fully integrate God's call into all areas of life. For followers of Christ, these secondary callings should lead us to our unique life purpose, to use our gifts and abilities to bring about flourishing for God's glory.[19]

Whelchel encourages us to "use our gifts and abilities to bring about flourishing for God's glory." We have been given gifts, let's use them! It is imperative that we use them in every sphere of our lives—church, family, community, and vocation. But, for the purposes of this booklet, we will focus on using our gifts and talents to serve the poor, empower the poor to fulfill their callings, and bring about flourishing in our churches and communities.

Regarding gifts and talents, as we strive to help others flourish we should have two aims. First, we must use our own gifts and talents, so that our efforts are effective. It is important for us to realize that these gifts are, in fact, *gifts* from God. We are to remain humble, knowing that our abilities "differ according to the grace given to us," as Paul states in Romans. However, it is important to recognize our gifts and humbly use them to serve our church and community, helping to fight poverty. We will be most effective when utilizing our gifts.

Second, we must cultivate the gifts and talents of those we are serving, so that our efforts are sustainable and respect the dignity of the poor. Both our gifts and the gifts of those we are coming alongside are important. Corbett and Fikkert reiterate that we must tailor our poverty-alleviation efforts to the gifts and talents of the poor. In *When Helping Hurts,* the authors write:

> The goal [of fighting poverty] is to see people restored to being what God created them to be: people who understand that they are created in the image of God with the gifts, abilities, and capacity to make decisions to effect change in the world around them; and people who steward their lives, communities, resources, and relationships in order to bring glory to God.[20]

Approaching poverty alleviation in a way that cultivates the gifts of others will, first and foremost, respect the dignity of the poor. It will help the poor feel fulfilled and valuable as they use their gifts and talents to realize their callings. And, it will provide sustainability as the poor recognize their gifts and cultivate new abilities.

Being created in God's image and the responsibility of carrying out the cultural mandate gives us purpose and direction for our lives. We must remember this truth and apply it to our poverty-fighting practice. Based on this biblical truth, we must respect, utilize, and grow the gifts and talents of the poor. We should utilize our own gifts and talents in doing so.

Poverty Is Not Just a Lack of Money

Biblical Truth 3: We are made for community.

Flourishing Principle 3: We must focus not only on the material, but also the social, spiritual, and psychological aspects of poverty.

The Christian faith worships a Triune God, one God in three persons—Father, Son, and Spirit. We read about the Trinity in the New Testament in stories such as Jesus's baptism (Matt. 3:13-17) and Jesus's discussions with the disciples during the last supper (John 14-16). The Trinity, although never mentioned explicitly in Scripture, is laid out specifically in the Great Commission, too: "Go therefore and make disciples of all nations, baptizing them in the name of the Father and of the Son and of the Holy Spirit" (Matt. 28:19).

God's Trinitarian nature also informs our understanding of what it means to be made in the image of God. God is in relationship with himself in the Trinity. In his book *Jesus the King*, Tim Keller describes the Trinity, writing,

> The Father, the Son, and the Spirit are each centering on the others, adoring and serving them…That's what God has been enjoying for all eternity. The Father, the Son, and the Spirit are pouring love and joy and adoration into the other, each one serving the other. They are infinitely seeking one another's glory, and so God is infinitely happy.[21]

Keller explains what this means for us:

> If this is ultimate reality, if this is what the God who made the universe is like, then this truth bristles and explodes with life-shaping, glorious implications for us. If this world was made by a triune God, *relationships of love* are what life is really all about (emphasis added).[22]

We have been made in God's image and exhibit his communicable attributes.[23] This understanding of the Trinity reveals that we have been designed as relational beings. We were made for community. With this insight, let's turn to a well-read passage with fresh eyes—1 Corinthians 12:12-27. This passage emphasizes our call to care for one another as a community:

Just as a body, though one, has many parts, but all its many parts form one body, so it is with Christ. For we were all baptized by one Spirit so as to form one body—whether Jews or Gentiles, slave or free—and we were all given the one Spirit to drink. Even so the body is not made up of one part but of many. Now if the foot should say, "Because I am not a hand, I do not belong to the body," it would not for that reason stop being part of the body. And if the ear should say, "Because I am not an eye, I do not belong to the body," it would not for that reason stop being part of the body. If the whole body were an eye, where would the sense of hearing be? If the whole body were an ear, where would the sense of smell be? But in fact God has placed the parts in the body, every one of them, just as he wanted them to be. If they were all one part, where would the body be? As it is, there are many parts, but one body. The eye cannot say to the hand, "I don't need you!" And the head cannot say to the feet, "I don't need you!" On the contrary, those parts of the body that seem to be weaker are indispensable, and the parts that we think are less honorable we treat with special honor. And the parts that are unpresentable are treated with special modesty, while our presentable parts need no special treatment. But God has put the body together, giving greater honor to the parts that lacked it, so that there should be no division in the body, but that its parts should have equal concern for each other. One part suffers, every part suffers with it; if one part is honored, every part rejoices with it. Now you are the body of Christ, and each one of you is a part of it.

This passage contains two main ideas. First, we all have a role to play in the body of Christ. We are made in the image of God and have inherent dignity and a purpose to glorify God in what we do. Our role matters, whether we think this role is big or small, important or insignificant, useful or boring. This is the idea of comparative advantage in economics—more is accomplished when people use their God-given gifts and talents to do what they do well, relative to other people. Comparative advantage creates more overall value because the costs of what we do are lower. The body of Christ functions properly and more efficiently if each person is using their God-given gifts to do what God has designed them to do.

The second idea is that as the members of the body suffer or rejoice, so the other members of the body suffer and rejoice, for we are all connected to and affect one another. What a beautiful picture of community! We are so connected as brothers and sisters of Christ that we impact one another. We celebrate with one another. We cry with one another. These relationships are incredibly significant because they are for our good and God's glory.

In the Trinity and in the body of Christ, we see that community is important. We were made for relationships because in them we can display God's glory. How does this relate to poverty? In an excerpt from the book *For the Least of These: A Biblical Answer to Poverty*, Peter Greer, president of HOPE International, explains what the word "poverty" means to the poor. He writes,

> In the 1990s, World Bank surveyed over sixty thousand of the financially poor throughout the developing world and how they described poverty. The poor did not focus on their material need; rather, they alluded to social and psychological aspects of poverty. Analyzing the study, Brian Fikkert and Steve Corbett of the Chalmers Center for Economic Development said, "Poor people typically talk in terms of shame, inferiority, powerlessness, humiliation, fear, hopelessness, depression, social isolation, and voicelessness." The study highlights that, by nature, poverty is innately social and psychological. In an informal survey, our clients at HOPE International in Rwanda affirmed that poverty is more than a lack of material possessions. In 2011, a lead trainer of a savings program in Rwanda posed a question to a group of twenty individuals within a savings group, most of whom lived on less than two dollars a day. 'How do you define poverty?' He asked. Listed below are their answers in the order provided:
>
> - Poverty is an empty heart
> - Not knowing your abilities and strengths
> - Not being able to make progress

- Isolation
- No hope or belief in yourself; knowing you can't take care of your family
- Broken relationships
- Not knowing God
- Not having basic things to eat; not having money
- Poverty is a consequence of not sharing
- Lack of good thoughts[24]

Poverty is not just a lack of money. It is not just hunger and need for shelter or clothing. Many poor people are plagued with social and spiritual poverty, and their view of their value is also affected.

Poverty Affects Relationships

The social aspects of poverty are just as important as the material. Imagine going through life alone—without any support structure, a family and friends to pick you up when you fall, or people you can rely on to ask for advice, encouragement, or accountability. This is how many of the poor described poverty in the list above:

> "Poverty is an empty heart." "Poverty is broken relationships." "Poverty is social isolation."[25]

Social poverty exacerbates material poverty. Most of us have options if we experience tough times. We can rely on family if we need to borrow money, crash on a friend's couch, or use our network's connections for a new job. Other people do not have these luxuries. What might be a bump in the road to someone with a support structure could be a mountain that derails a poor person. We are made to enjoy, rely on, and reflect God's glory through relationships. Seeing that poverty is more than just a lack of material resources changes the way we work for people's flourishing.

Poverty Stems from Separation from God

Further, we see elements of spiritual poverty in the list above.

> "Poverty is hopelessness." "Poverty is not knowing God." "Poverty is powerlessness."[26]

Our relationships with others are important; our relationship with the Lord is even more so. We usually only consider material poverty, but the Bible often discusses the spiritually poor—those who do not know God. Spiritual poverty, in the sense of not knowing God, affects the way people view their dignity, their purpose, and the world. It is important to keep spiritual poverty in mind as we serve the poor. Without a relationship with Jesus, people cannot fully know hope, grace, and love.

As Christians, we believe that to fully flourish we must understand how we fit into the bigger picture. God created this world and everything in it. Mankind disobeyed God and we were separated from him. But, in God's mercy, he sent us his son Jesus, who is fully God and fully man. He lived a perfect life, died on the cross as a sacrifice for our sins, and rose from the grave three days later, defeating death. When we trust in Jesus, we can be reconciled to God. One day, Jesus will return and those who trust in him will spend eternal life in God's presence. We must know these truths, so that we can understand and fulfill our purpose to glorify God.

Poverty Affects Peoples' Self-Worth
Finally, in the definitions of poverty above we also see psychological effects of poverty.

> "Poverty is not knowing your abilities and strengths." "Poverty is no hope or belief in yourself." "Poverty is shame." "Poverty is inferiority." "Poverty is humiliation." "Poverty is fear."[27]

According to these quotes, poverty often corrupts the poor's view of their dignity and value. Though this is not always the case with the poor, many have been torn down in their relationships, not built up by them. They have been treated in such a way that they feel they are worth nothing. Many do not believe they have gifts and talents. There can be a sense of shame about where they are in life and fear about what might come next.

These concerns certainly overlap with spiritual poverty. If a person knows Christ, but is materially poor, they may not experience this type of poverty, for they know their strength, worth, and dignity come from Christ. For Christians, these psychological responses to poverty are lies that contradict Scripture. A better understanding of and obedience to Scripture combats these lies without changing the poor's material circumstances.

That said, we must keep in mind the psychological effects of poverty when serving the poor because these effects impact the way a person will interact with the people and organizations that want to serve them. It is essential to help the poor understand they have dignity and capability. We should walk alongside them, cultivating their gifts and talents. Our goal is to help them understand they have value and can care for themselves and those around them.

Whereas charity only works to alleviate the poor's material poverty, to truly be effective, we must consider *all* aspects of poverty, the material *and* the social, spiritual, and psychological.

Learning to Love in a Helpful Way

As we try to show love by helping others flourish, we must find the most effective, helpful ways. Our love should not harm those we are trying to serve. Good intentions are not enough. We need to look not only at the immediate circumstances, but also serve the poor in the long-run, discouraging dependence and encouraging sustainability. Given our definition of poverty, we desire for a poor person to have more suitable options. Using what we've learned so far, we want people to:

- Understand that they have dignity and feel like they are treated with respect
- Use their gifts and talents to live out their calling
- Live with a support structure without social isolation
- Know the gospel

Traditionally, churches have approached poverty alleviation with charity. We might run a food bank, donate clothing, or fly to Nicaragua to paint an orphanage. Does that meet our principles? Does it propel the poor toward a life with more options, dignity, social support, and fulfillment from using their talents? No. While the poor's immediate needs may be met, this process can breed lack of self-worth, dependency, or even entitlement. It does not help relationships form, and it does-n't allow the poor to use their gifts and talents. This approach to fighting poverty is not a sustainable and effective way to help the poor flourish.

Corbett and Fikkert write, "The way that we act toward the economically poor often communicates—albeit unintentionally—that we are superior and they are inferior."[28] This style of "helping" others can shatter a person's sense of self-worth. They do not think they have dignity, and they do not feel respected. As they re-ceive free food and free clothing over and over, they start to depend on this source of resources, and this dependence can turn into entitlement. They still live in so-cial isolation, and their gifts and talents are not utilized.

Lupton reiterates the message that traditional charity is not working to lift peo-ple out of poverty. He writes, "For all our efforts to eliminate poverty—our enti-tlements, our programs, our charities—we have succeeded only in creating a permanent underclass, dismantling their family structures, and eroding their ethic of work. And our poor continue to become poorer."[29]

Let's try something else. Let's use our biblical truths and flourishing principles to fight poverty in a different way. Let's take steps towards dignity and support structures and fulfillment. Let's not just put a Band-Aid on the problem, but jump into the messiness of fighting poverty and walk alongside the poor as we try to find ways that we can flourish more together. Let's truly love our neighbors.

CHAPTER 3: **APPLICATION: MICRO WORK LEADS TO MACRO CHANGE**

I n the last section, we learned three flourishing principles based on biblical truths. Let's now see how three organizations are actively putting these principles into action. There are dozens more organizations who are doing development work in a sustainable, effective way. But, we can't discuss them all in this booklet. The goal for this section is to highlight the variety of ways the flourishing principles can inform the way we work for flourishing to make a difference in our communities.

As we review these organizations, one practical application will serve as our guiding theme—micro work can lead to macro change. By serving the poor in our communities, we are helping at the individual, micro level, but the impact doesn't stop there. When people across the country and the world do their part to serve the poor in their communities, it will cause effects at the societal, macro level.

We can't always solve a societal problem with service at the individual level. Sometimes a macro, systemic shift is needed to make big changes. However, we *can* always make a difference by serving and loving our neighbors. While we are not able or called to solve all poverty, this part of the booklet will show you how people are sustainably and effectively making a difference through relationships at the individual level.

Let's see how this plays out at Jobs for Life, STEP Richmond, and Tearfund.

Jobs for Life

In a recent blog, David Spickard, president and CEO of Jobs for Life (JfL) discusses how jobs can serve the neediest in our communities. He tells a story of two young women, "April" and "Mandy." Both women grew up in abusive homes and ran away. Both were young and didn't have the marketable skills to find a steady job. Hopeless, abused, and dejected, April and Mandy turned to selling their bodies to survive.[30] As Ann McAdams notes in a report on human trafficking, "Experts say 90% of [children in the US sex-trafficking industry] were sexually abused as children."[31]

Spickard reflects on their stories saying, "Both April and Mandy say they want to stop, but when? *'If I can find a job,' April says...* As I stared into space, I couldn't get those **six words** out of my mind. A job would make her stop? That's it?" (emphasis his).[32] He continues, wondering about other massive social problems. Could jobs help with poverty and crime rates? Could solid jobs help with domestic violence? What about homelessness? He ends his blog stating, "Issues like these are way too complex to fix with one simple idea. It's not just about a job. People are trapped, systems are broken, perpetrators are cruel, and darkness is real. Solutions take patience, time, relentless courage, and unwavering faith. And yet the doorway out of oppression and injustice often is marked by the assurance of dignity and hope found through God's gift of work."[33]

JfL is an organization that focuses on helping the jobless find, be prepared for, and keep a job. By working at the individual level with the jobless, big transformations happen not only in an individual's life, but also in the lives around them. This micro work can cause a macro change, just as Spickard ponders in his blog.

JfL encourages and equips the poor by coming alongside the jobless with a job-preparedness training curriculum. The training is biblically based, church-led, relationship-centered, and character-driven.[34] Let's look at each of these aspects of their curriculum to see how they relate to our flourishing principles.

As we learned earlier, our purpose in life is to image God and to fulfill the cultural mandate. We do this by using our gifts and talents that he has given us to fulfill his purposes. For the jobless, not having a job disconnects them from their purpose and their sense of value. They find themselves unable to provide for their family and feeling unimportant to society. The biblically based and church-led aspects of the job-preparedness curriculum assist the poor in taking a step toward finding a job, but also connect the poor to the larger story and purpose of their lives in Christ. This combats not only material poverty, but also spiritual and psychological poverty.

The curriculum is also relationship-based. Each JfL student is paired with a mentor who provides guidance and is a listening ear through the process. By forming a relationship with the student, the mentor is better equipped to tailor the program to the student's needs and strengths, cultivating their gifts and talents. These relationships also address the social aspects of the student's poverty.

The character-driven aspect of the job-prep training provides sustainability. By focusing on a student's character, they are more marketable for any job. They learn things like timeliness and teamwork as well as respecting leadership and approaches for overcoming obstacles. The well-rounded approach of this curriculum is harder than just connecting someone to a job, or giving them enough money or resources to subsist. However, this approach, because it is sustainable, is a better way to love and serve the jobless community.

Statistics back up the important role of jobs in the fight against poverty, as we read in *Income and Poverty in the United States*, a 2014 report on poverty in the United States written by Carmen DeNavas-Walt and Bernadette D. Proctor. While these statistics use a definition of poverty that only accounts for material aspects of poverty, this data is helpful in giving us an idea of the change in poverty over time. This report states that of the percentage of Americans who did not work at least one week in 2014, 32.7 percent were in poverty. However, of the percentage of people who worked at some point in 2014 for any given length of time, only 7 percent were below the poverty threshold. Of the percentage of people who worked full-time, year round, only 3 percent were below the poverty threshold.[35]

These statistics paint a picture for us—connecting the poor with a job is a proven method to decrease poverty. Yet, traditional efforts to serve the poor through charity are far more popular in the local church, such as giving away food, clothing, and shelter. David Bass, in his book *Clearing Obstacles to Work*, writes, "Of America's 460,000 churches, 62 percent give away food, but only 2 percent encourage work as a more permanent, effective, and dignified means of alleviating poverty."[36] When we participate in these traditional efforts, how often have we met the folks we are trying to help and developed a relationship to support them in a sustainable way?

JfL is striving to change this, turning this statistic on its head and encouraging churches to take part in fighting for flourishing by connecting the poor with jobs. Imagine what a difference it would make if 62 percent of US churches had JfL programs rather than food pantries.

Let's return to Spickard's reflections. How can the act of helping one person find a job affect the massive problems our society faces? People with jobs have a more sustainable income, which decreases their chances of poverty and homelessness. There are studies that link employment with decreased property crime.[37] In the case of domestic abuse, women are more able to break away from their toxic environment if they have a job and can support themselves and their children. Fewer women like "April" and "Mandy" will get misled into the sex-trafficking industry if they have more opportunities for work. While it may seem like a simple fix, connecting the poor to jobs can be transformative. If people across this country help others find solid jobs that give them dignity and the ability to support themselves, these micro connections will have a massive macro impact, changing the landscape of poverty.

Beyond this, jobs *create value* for a community. Businesses provide people with goods and services they want and need. More jobs mean more value and better access for the poor to what they need. And, connecting people with jobs in a given neighborhood increases the income of that neighborhood. This extra money is poured into businesses in the area, creating more wealth for the community. This can start a snowball effect—leading to more jobs, more income, more creation, and more thriving. We should keep in mind that it is important to not only connect the poor to jobs, but also to create jobs in poor areas. Along with our poverty fighting approach at the individual level, we should advocate for macro conditions that foster an environment that allows for and encourages businesses in poorer parts of our communities to thrive.

The JfL approach creates sustainable change in the community because it respects the dignity of the poor, addresses the manifold aspects of poverty, and utilizes the poor's God-given gifts and talents. The poor own their own development.

JfL fights for flourishing on the individual level in a way that can have huge implications for the communities they are working in.

JfL has put together a model that helps the poor champion their own flourishing. Their training program meets our three flourishing principles.

- JfL respects their students' dignity and changes the way their students view themselves through the curriculum
- Job placement provides students with a means to care for themselves and utilizes their gifts and talents
- The program also connects students with a mentor and a community of believers
- This process encourages students to take part in their own development, making the changes in their lives sustainable

STEP Richmond

In the heart of Richmond, VA looms Gilpin Court, a housing project 783 units large. I grew up in a suburb west of Richmond. If I was planning to drive into the city for an evening, I remember my parents saying things like, "Well just make sure you don't end up near Gilpin Court!" or "You can't go there; that's too close to Gilpin Court." As Edwin Slipek Jr. writes in his article, "The Lost Neighborhood," many have called it the "city's most isolated and desperate neighborhood."[38]

Gilpin Court is the largest housing project in the city, located in the North Jackson Ward. According to Slipek:

- "80 percent of [Gilipin Court's] households fall below the poverty line of $15,000"
- "65 percent of its adult population didn't finish high school"
- "fewer than 1 percent of the population has a college degree"[39]

Ironically, Gilpin Court was built in 1943 as a solution to the poverty of the area. It replaced previous dilapidated housing and was supposed to jump-start the economy. This is an example of an attempt at fighting poverty that was not only unsuccessful, but detrimental to the community. Slipek writes, "In other places [in Richmond], the combined stew of people, nature, commerce, recreation, architecture, and cultural and educational institutions melds and flows with at least some natural synergy."[40] But, apart from Gilpin Court there are only thirty-four houses and a high-rise building for seniors in North Jackson Ward.[41] There is a strip of decrepit businesses and houses that have long since been vacated. By filling the entire area with subsidized housing, Gilpin Court chased out all possibility of a thriving economy. Neighborhoods need this mixing and "melding" of institutions as described by Slipek to thrive.

What can we do for neighborhoods like North Jackson Ward? Top-down, macro solutions, such as subsidized housing projects, only worsen the problem. Let's consider another approach—one marked by assistance at the individual level that addresses more than just the material aspects of poverty. We will again see that micro solutions can bring about macro effects. Strategies to Elevate People (STEP) Richmond exists to serve the people living in Gilpin Court. Their mission is to "develop strategies to meet the needs of the urban poor in Richmond."[42] STEP works with the church, as an arm of the church to serve the poor. They emphasize that each person is a significant part of the body of Christ and realize the need for relationships to promote flourishing. And, they stress education and work as means to help the poor use their gifts and talents to contribute to sustainable change in their community.[43]

To achieve their mission, they have a variety of programs. They are a JfL Network site, so they partner with a local church to provide JfL's job preparedness curriculum to the residents of Gilpin Court. They also have a reading program and summer enrichment programs. These programs help further the student's education, and volunteers serve as mentors to the children. Community events and a Christmas store are also important pieces of their outreach.[44] We have already learned how JfL is transformative for the poor. Let's look at the other programs to see how they fit our flourishing principles and are effective methods for serving the poor.

Education and Mentorship

STEP's Victory Reading Program is an after-school program in which volunteers help students complete their homework and practice their reading skills; students also have a time for snack and they do a devotion with volunteers. This seems so simple, but education and mentorship can have a transformative impact on students.

Here is what some of the parents of the kids in the program say about the program:

- "The program is just outstanding…it gives the kids an edge in the classroom."
- "My daughter had…math problems, and my son—he has a lot of little attitude problems. So I've seen a whole lot of progress."
- "My daughter was failing in English due to she wasn't reading in the classroom, so we put her in the program. She liked it… they taught her more how to read and she just does it now!"
- "They have a 'Yes, you can!' attitude with the children. 'Yes, you can spell this word!' 'Yes, you can read!' It gives them a confidence that they wouldn't ordinarily have."
- "I see the results. When they go outside, you can see the difference, you know, that somebody besides mom and dad care about them."[45]

In Gilpin Court, 96 percent of the tenants are single-mother households, and there are 550 children under the age of five.[46] The children are not always supervised or guided; having men and women in their lives that aren't their parents, who care for them and mentor them can help them feel valued, respected, and give them a sense of direction. For this reason, mentorship relationships are essential for poor youth and teens. These statistics from the National Mentoring Partnership (NMP) show us how mentorship is effective:

- "45 percent of all at-risk youth with a mentor are enrolled in some type of postsecondary education as opposed to 29 percent of at-risk youth who are enrolled but never had a mentor."[47]
- "At-risk young adults with a mentor are more likely to report participating regularly in sports or extracurricular activities (67 percent of at-risk youth with mentors compared to 37 percent of those without them). These

activities translate into the higher self-esteem and self-confidence that are necessary traits for youth to engage in teamwork and community work, and to be successful in life."[48]

Mentorship is successful because it targets all aspects of poverty. By bringing together a mentor and mentee, a relationship is formed, and the mentor is more aware of how best to walk alongside the mentee. This is an essential step in the process of helping a youth or teen grow in their sense of worth, sense of dignity, and their idea of self-reliance. The mentor, through this relationship, better understands the mentee's gifts and talents and can help cultivate these gifts. As a result, you see a higher drive for the future. The mentee is statistically more likely to go to college and engage in extracurricular activities. Another statistic from the NMP report shows us that mentees are more likely to be engaged in leadership roles and volunteering in the community.[49]

Beyond mentorship, the Victory Reading Program provides a safe space for the students after school. It helps students do their homework and sharpens their reading skills. Education is also essential for development. Brian Jacob and Jens Ludwig write, "One of the best ways to avoid being poor as an adult is to obtain a good education. People who have higher levels of academic achievement and more years of schooling earn more than those with lower levels of human capital."[50] Poor students need a good education to rise out of cyclical poverty. Yet, public schools in poor neighborhoods have few resources and are notorious for an environment that is not conducive to learning. The reading program is a way for students to get extra one-on-one attention and practice their skills in small groups with a supportive leader. Programs like this can be a way that students' education is supplemented.

In the same way that connecting the poor with a job on the individual level can lead to decreased poverty, homelessness, and property crime, we see that higher levels of education can help prevent poverty as well as violent crime and high prison rates. One study reports "College education is important in predicting homicide rates among all three racial groups [assessed in the study], with the proportion of these populations with a college education exhibiting a significant inverse association with the homicide rate."[51] Engaging in mentorship and tutoring, gives poor children a hand up, equipping them to fight for their own flourishing as they strive to break the cycle of poverty in their communities.

The Christmas Store and Applications for Your Church

Beyond mentorship and education, STEP Richmond runs a Christmas store that sells toys at a discount to poor families at Christmastime. This store might sound weird to you. If you've ever participated in a toy drive that gives gifts to the poor, you may even think this idea sounds wrong.

Look past the surface of toy drives and see some less-noticed effects of these donations. Lupton recounts his experience with Christmas donations. Countless times, he donated and organized Christmas toy drop-offs. But, in 1981, he had just moved into a poor neighborhood, and got to see this act of charity from another perspective. He writes,

> When the knock finally came on their front door, their mom greeted the visitors—a well-dressed family with young children—and invited them to step inside. A nervous smile concealed her embarrassment as she graciously accepted armfuls of neatly wrapped gifts. In the commotion, no one noticed that the children's father had quietly slipped out of the room—no one but their mom... I was witnessing a side I had never noticed before: how a father is emasculated in his own home in front of his wife and children for not being able to provide presents for his family...[52]

It is kind and compassionate to provide a Christmas gift for a child in need. But, we must consider unintended consequences. In this story, the family bringing gifts made the poor childrens' Christmas sweeter, but at the cost of embarrassing the parents. This may seem like a small price to pay, and many may believe that the parents should be less prideful or that regardless of embarrassment someone should step in and provide gifts for the kids since the parents can't. But what does this say to the poor family?

1. As the children wait for the well-off family to come with their presents, they are learning that the rich will take care of the poor. The rich family comes every year to bring gifts. The childrens' attitude may change from thankful to expectant to entitled. This act teaches the children to wait for someone else to provide for them, taking away their dignity to provide for themselves. It can make them feel like recipients in life rather than active participants.

2. The parents may be embarrassed but thankful that another family has provided for their children. In our second flourishing principle, we discussed the importance of our callings to church, community, work, and family. The well-intentioned, well-off family is taking away the parents' opportunity to provide for their family. The poor family feels reliant on strangers, and valueless to their family and society. This disrespects their dignity.

STEP has another approach. They ask for donations for Christmas gifts, but sell them at their Christmas store at half price or less. Again, you may protest—"now the kids will get fewer gifts, and it forces the parents to spend their limited money on Christmas gifts!" But, this method respects the dignity of the poor. It allows the parents to live out their calling to work and provide for the family. The parents can work hard, save up, and come to the Christmas store to buy their children Christmas gifts. The shoppers can afford the gifts because the Christmas store is run by donations and toys are sold at a steep discount.

This is only a minor tweak from the old system, but look at the massive implications! Those who have means are still able to make donations and serve the poor during Christmas. The children are still able to receive gifts. The parents have ownership over the gifts they get to buy for their kids. Imagine the feeling of dignity and self-worth that comes from being able to pick out your children's Christmas gifts instead of relying on handouts. Imagine the parent as they watch their children's faces light up when they see gifts under the tree on Christmas morning, and how proud the parents feel knowing they could provide for their family in this way. The Christmas store method communicates the importance of being an active participant in their own development. This is the message we want poverty-fighting programs to send.

This is an important takeaway from the story of STEP Richmond that you can apply to your church or a nonprofit you are involved with. Does your church have a food bank? Have food bank customers pay a small amount or work in the pantry, so they can shop for food with a sense of dignity. Do you volunteer at a clothing closet? Sell the clothes at a discount, rather than just giving them away. Does your church volunteer to serve dinner to the homeless? Don't just have church members plan, make, and serve the dinner. Involve those you are serving. Have them help brainstorm dinner ideas. Split them up into a team that helps serve dinner and a team that does the dishes. Mix the volunteers and homeless clients together so that they can form bonds and treat one another with mutual respect.

These are small tweaks, but think of the difference they could make. These programs say "you have gifts and talents and we encourage you to use them" rather than "you are not capable of doing anything, let me just take care of this." By modifying traditional charity routes, we can channel our compassion in a way that respects the dignity of the poor and addresses the social, psychological, and spiritual aspects of poverty.

STEP Richmond will not be able to change the nature of Gilpin Court. It will still be a place that people run from rather than flock to. The institutions in place are working against the poor in this area. North Jackson Ward needs businesses and diversity to be transformed. But, STEP Richmond is doing what it can to serve the least of these in a devastated neighborhood. By working at the individual level, investing in people's lives, STEP transforms its community from the inside out. This change of culture makes it a better place to live and works with the poor right where they are. Changing institutions is essential, but we can't wait until the institutions change to start making a difference. Let's let our micro work encourage the macro change.

STEP Richmond's programs meet our three flourishing principles.

- Jobs for Life
  - Meets principles as discussed above.

- Mentorship and education
  - ○ Helps kids develop their gifts and talents, respecting their dignity and value
  - ○ Supplies kids with meaningful mentor relationships that can heal aspects of social and psychological poverty and allow for individualized, sustainable development
  - ○ Provides kids with daily devotions, targeting spiritual poverty

- Christmas store
  - ○ Provides parents accessible options for Christmas gifts, giving them the dignity of picking out and providing their children with gifts for Christmas at affordable prices
  - ○ Allows parents the opportunity to provide for their family, living out their call to family

Tearfund

Tearfund is a U.K.-based nonprofit that works with poor communities across the globe. They understand that there is more to poverty than just material needs. They approach poverty in a way that encourages the community to pull itself out of poverty. Here is how they describe why their organization exists:

> When a community lifts itself out of poverty, everything changes. Poverty does more than exhaust, starve, trap and kill people. It destroys their sense of worth, limits their horizons, robs people of the chance to reach their full potential…We do whatever it takes to end poverty and rebuild poor communities. We work through local churches, because they're Jesus' body on earth, ready to care for the whole person—and the whole community—inside and out.[53]

Tearfund has a holistic approach to fighting poverty. They have a four-pronged mission:

1. Serve those in the greatest need—including poor communities, marginalized groups, vulnerable adults, and children.
2. Strive to support lasting, local change—utilizing the local church, community empowerment, and education, while focusing on the whole person.

3. Fight against global issues, such as conflict, disasters, HIV, injustice, and climate change.

4. Providing access to life's essentials—food, clean water and toilets, health care, and livelihoods.[54]

Tearfund provides aid for those in crisis. For those who are in cyclical poverty, Tearfund focuses on development so that the global poor can experience sustainable changes in their communities. Let's look at a primary way that Tearfund works in poor communities—"self-help groups."

Meseret's Story

Meet Meseret—she's a wife and mom of three children in Ethiopia.[55] Before joining a self-help group, Meseret and her family were barely surviving on her husband's wages as a laborer. She and her husband were not able to provide enough food for their children.

Meseret heard of the self-help group at the local church in her community. She approached the group looking for some handout help, but instead got connected with her own self-help group. A self-help group saves money together, and gives microloans to the members of its group. Meseret's group started saving 50 cents a week. This approach encourages a community to utilize their own resources, knowledge, and talents to create a way for themselves to fight poverty. Employing innovation and utilizing market systems, the women in the self-help group come up with new ways to support their community and make a profit, so they can provide for their families. The group promotes flourishing for both the women participating and the community through new microbusinesses.

Meseret received a small loan from her self-help group and started selling charcoal. Using the profits, she started making and selling handicrafts. Now she is saving up to start a hairdressing shop using the profits from her handicrafts. She and her husband have enough money to provide three meals a day for their family, and they just recently were even able to replace the roof on their house. Here is how Meseret describes her experience with her self-help group:

> I can't express in words what my group means to me. They are my sisters—we support each other in everything. And we help to look after the rest of the community. By saving and investing in small businesses, I was able to completely transform my life and give my daughters a better future.[56]

Meseret describes her relationship with her self-help group in a similar way that we described poverty—that it has not only material effects, but also the psychological, social, and spiritual. Her self-help group helped her gather capital to start a microbusiness to help her provide for herself and her family. But, it also helped her feel a sense of worth, provided her with a community, and opened her eyes to Christ. She is now a believer and is active in her local church.[57]

In Meseret's description of her self-help group we see aspects of the early church as described in Acts 2: 42-47:

> They devoted themselves to the apostles' teaching and to fellowship, to the breaking of bread and to prayer. Everyone was filled with awe at the many wonders and signs performed by the apostles. All the believers were together and had everything in common. They sold property and possessions to give to anyone who had need. Every day they continued to meet together in the temple courts. They broke bread in their homes and ate together with glad and sincere hearts, praising God and enjoying the favor of all the people. And the Lord added to their number daily those who were being saved.

The early church was dedicated to learning more about God and spending time in community and in prayer. They voluntarily shared possessions, lived sacrificially for their community, and praised God for what they were learning from the apostles. Often, people take this passage to support a top-down approach where the government redistributes money from the rich to the poor. However, Meseret's story is a more fitting example of how to live out Acts 2-5—a voluntary community that serves one another sacrificially, spends time learning about and praying to God together, and works together in micro ways to promote flourishing in their whole community.

Local Knowledge

Meseret's story gives us just a glimpse of how Tearfund works with poor communities. The self-help group was guided by Tearfund-trained staff, but otherwise relied on local knowledge, talent, and resources to accomplish sustainable changes in their community. Tearfund's service in Ethiopia is sustainable because the poor have ownership over their development and can use their gifts and talents to make a difference in their community. Tearfund's approach addresses our flourishing principles.

One of the most significant lessons we learn from Tearfund is the importance of using local knowledge. This type of knowledge is based on the local culture and is developed over time by seeing what works and what does not work for a community given their resources, constraints, strengths, and weaknesses. Tearfund relies on local knowledge to cater their poverty-fighting tactics to the needs and culture of that community. They partner with local churches and local nonprofits that utilize this knowledge to transform communities. The people who are living in poverty day in and day out are the experts, and have a better understanding of what is needed in their community to develop.

Local knowledge is the reason why this booklet focuses primarily on domestic poverty. Tearfund utilizes the idea of employing local knowledge to help the global poor. It connects churches in the developing world with churches in the developed world in an effective way. This organization, and organizations like it, make it possible for us to serve the global poor in a way that is helpful, not hurtful.

Think back to my story about the fundraiser for clean water in Malawi. I don't know where the raised funds went, much less if the money helped people. In *For the Least of These*, Peter Greer tells a story about "PlayPumps," which were the newest Western solution to Africa's water problem. Organizations would come in, build a well, and cover it with a merry-go-round. The idea is that the kids could play on the merry-go-round and it would pump the water out as it spun. Eventually, most these PlayPumps broke. The merry-go-rounds covered the villages' only water source, leaving the villages worse off than before.[58]

This is a common story—organizations come in, build a water pump, and leave. They do this out of compassion and with good intentions. But, they do not train the village in how to maintain the water source. When (and if) they come back, they fix the pump, and leave again. This causes a sense of dependency among the villagers. Lupton recounts a conversation he had with Juan Ulloa, director of Opportunity International's branch in Nicaragua. Ulloa explains the problem with church donations coming from the United States and their impact on his communities' version of self-help groups. Juan says, "They destroy the initiative of my people... People say 'Why should we borrow money when the churches give it to us?"[59] Instead of relying on donations, the poor need a sense of ownership to bring about sustained development in their community.

It is not wrong to want to provide fresh water to those who do not have it—I certainly was trying to help when I hosted the fundraising carnival. We must learn how to do this in a way that gives the poor dignity and uses their gifts to create, maintain, and sustain the solution. Local knowledge matters. Had the villagers been given the opportunity to weigh in on the best method for fresh water, they wouldn't have ended up with a merry-go-round blocking their only water source. Tearfund is showing us how we can partake in global poverty alleviation in a way that can truly help those we are trying to serve.

At the same time, local knowledge teaches us that we are best equipped to serve the poor in our own backyard. We better understand the culture of our community. We are aware of networks, organizations, and churches that can assist the poor. We can build stronger relationships with the poor in our community to utilize their local knowledge to encourage sustained change. These advantages will make us stronger advocates for flourishing in our own community. This is the idea behind asset-based community development (ABCD), which starts a change in a community by assessing and employing the residents' gifts and talents. Corbett and Fikkert tell a story about conducting an asset inventory of a community. Fikkert was going door to door in a housing project with the goal of learning the local knowledge and talent of the community. Here is a piece of his conversation at one door:

I tried not to flinch and launched into my sales pitch, "Hello, I am from Community Presbyterian Church…We are conducting a survey today to find out what gifts God has placed in this community. What skills and abilities do you have?" [The woman at the door] said, "What?!" looking even more incredulous than before… I swallowed hard and repeated, "What skills do you have? What are you good at doing?"…The lady said sheepishly, "Well, I guess I can cook." Suddenly, a voice from the dark unknown behind the lady shouted out, "She can cook chittlins like there is no tomorrow!" Another voice yelled, "Yeah, ain't nobody can cook as good as she can!" Slowly a smile spread across her face and she said, "Yes, I think I can cook."

Next thing I knew I found myself sitting in the living room with about six African Americans gathered around… "This is Joe; he can fix bikes. Whenever one of the kids in the project has a bike that needs fixing, Joe is the man." A smile spread across Joe's face. "And this here is Mac. How is your car running? If you ever have trouble with your car, bring it right here to Mac." I noticed that Mac started to sit up a little straighter in his chair. They went on and on bragging about one another to me.[60]

Approaching poverty alleviation in this way meets our three principles—it gives the poor a sense of dignity, utilizes their gifts and talents, and approaches the multiple aspects of poverty. ABCD harnesses local knowledge by starting with the poor's assets rather than their needs. It is a humble approach that puts the emphasis on the poor's gifts rather than the gifts of those fighting poverty, which respects the poor's dignity. We, the ones trying to help the poor, are limited, and we must rely on local knowledge and the poor's gifts and talents to help them create sustainable change within their community.

Local knowledge and talent is essential in the fight against poverty, whether it is employed in our own community or across the globe. Tearfund combines local knowledge with compassionate gifts and service of people in other countries to serve the global poor effectively and sustainably. Comparing their methods with those of a group like PlayPumps shows you the dramatic difference between charity and development and contrasts the prideful way of relying on our own knowledge vs. humbly employing local knowledge.

Tearfund addresses our three flourishing principles:

- Self-help groups, when done in a church setting, address the many aspects of poverty—material, social, psychological, and spiritual.
- Utilizing local knowledge in global communities gives the poor dignity and allows them to use their gifts and talents to create value and fight poverty.
- Local knowledge and self-help groups provide opportunities for sustainable development.

From jobs to mentorship to self-help groups, we have seen a variety of ways the flourishing principles can be put into action in fighting poverty in a sustainable, effective way. Each organization respects the dignity of the poor by allowing them to be at the source of change. The organizations don't just focus on material poverty or giving handouts. These programs utilize the poor's gifts and talents and address all aspects of poverty in some way. They focus on fighting poverty in relationship, and over the long-term. While their work is a difficult, long process, it is the most effective way to truly love our neighbors and encourage sustainable change for the poor.

CHAPTER 4: **GROUP EXERCISE**

This section will guide you through four steps to determine how you can best serve the poor in your community. It can be done on your own, but is best done with a group.

Each step has five parts. "Pray" prompts you to go to the Lord as you start this process of planning to effectively serve the poor. It readies your heart and mind. "Reflect" is designed to be done on your own. Your answers to the reflection questions provide a foundation for the next section. "Discuss" builds on your answers in the reflection section by providing several questions to discuss as a group. If you are working alone, answer the discussion questions as you would the reflection questions, or grab a friend to work through the questions with. "Write" allows you to summarize what you have learned. There is no specific way you should write—you can use bullet points or write your summary in paragraph format. The point of this section is to provide yourself with a review of that step, so that you can utilize it in later steps. Finally, "Resources" provides helpful websites, reports, and activities to guide you in the process.

STEP 1: What are the needs in your community?

The goal of step one is to get the conversation started. It will give you time to assess the main issues you see in your community. You will analyze the causes of these problems and start brainstorming how these problems can be addressed. By the end of step one, you will have a description of the poverty landscape in your community.

Pray

Ask the Lord to open your eyes to the needs of your community. Pray that he will guide you along this process, helping you see the problems he wants you to take action to fix. Pray for the poor in your community. Boldly ask God to intervene, using you and others around you to come alongside the poor and help set them on the path toward flourishing.

Reflect
1. List three to five main problems the poor in your community face.
2. List three to five root causes of each problem.

Take your time answering these questions. Do your research. Use the resources below as a good starting place for answering these questions. Reflect on what you see around you and common concerns about your community you hear discussed at work, in your classes, or at church.

Discuss
1. How are your lists similar? How are they different?
2. For the variety of problems listed, do some of the root causes overlap?
3. Keeping the flourishing principles and the causes of the problems in mind, what are some ways to address the problems?

Write
Describe the poverty landscape of your community. Include major problems, sources of these problems, and preliminary ideas of how to tackle these issues.

Resources
- **Family**—Family Research Council's Belonging Index Report— http://downloads.frc.org/EF/EF10L25.pdf
- **Faith**—Pew Forum Religious Landscape Survey— http://www.pewforum.org/religious-landscape-study/
- **Hunger**—Feeding America—list of top states with food insecurity— http://www.feedingamerica.org/hunger-in-america/impact-of-hunger/hunger-and-poverty/hunger-and-poverty-fact-sheet.html
- **Homelessness**—The State of Homelessness in America, 2015 Report— http://www.endhomelessness.org/page/-/files/State_of_Homelessness_2015_FINAL_online.pdf
- **Jobless**—Bureau of Labor Statistics— http://www.bls.gov/web/laus/laumstrk.htm

STEP 2: What are your gifts and talents?

As we discussed in Chapter 3, the concept of comparative advantage in economics says that more is accomplished when people use their God-given gifts and talents to do what they do well relative to other people. In this section, you will discover your comparative advantage for fighting poverty by analyzing your strengths and passions.

Pray

Ask the Lord to make known to you the gifts he has given you. Pray that he would give you a humble heart as he shows you your strengths. Ask for wisdom for using your talents in your efforts to alleviate poverty. Pray also that the Lord would show the poor their gifts and talents, and guide them in using these strengths to fight poverty.

Reflect

1. What are you good at? What do you think you do well? What have other people told you they think you do well? Do you have tangible examples?
2. What do you like doing?
3. What motivates you? What is your passion? What raises your emotions? Do you feel called to fight poverty in any specific way?
4. How much time do you have to offer?
5. Optional activities—Do the *Discover Your Story* activity and take the StrengthsFinder and Myers Briggs assessments as described in the Resources section below.

Discuss

1. Working with a partner or in a small group, discuss gifts you see in your group members. Provide specific examples of how you've seen these gifts in action.
2. If you have done the optional activities, discuss your results from the StrengthsFinder and Myers Briggs tests and finish the activity in the *Discover Your Story* guide in your small group.
3. Back in a large group, share what you learned in the smaller groups.

4. Discuss how the group members' gifts complement and overlap with one another.

5. If you want to volunteer together as a group, are there specific ways this group is gifted overall? Is there something unique about this group or number of people that can be helpful in a certain way?

Write

Describe your comparative advantage in fighting poverty. Include the type of poverty you are targeting, what types of roles would be ideal for your gifts, how much time you can invest, and any considerations for unique group involvement.

Resources

- *Discover Your Story* guide—This guide discusses the idea of calling, and contains an activity that helps you assess your gifts, talents, and motivations. The activity is perfect to do in a group of two to three people. The goal is to better understand what you like to do and why you like to do it.

- Clifton StrengthsFinder—This test allows you to recognize your top strengths. Gallup describes it in this way: "Clifton StrengthsFinder results give people a way to discuss and develop their unique combination of skills, talents, and knowledge—also known as strengths." https://www.gallupstrengthscenter.com/

- Myers Briggs—This test helps you better understand your personality type. The Myers & Briggs Foundation describes the assessment in this way: "It gives you a framework for understanding yourself and appreciating the differences in others." https://www.mbtionline.com/[61]

STEP 3: What mechanisms already exist for sustainable service?

There are countless churches and organizations that are working with the poor in an effective, sustainable way. This step will help you think through what is already happening in your community and how you can be involved.

Pray

Pray for God's guidance as you contemplate how to get involved in fighting poverty in your community. Ask the Lord to use the ministries and organizations in your community to empower the poor and encourage flourishing. Pray against any unintended harm ministries and organizations may cause, and ask for guidance for the leadership of these organizations.

Reflect

1. What are some ways your church is already trying to bring about flourishing in your community?
2. What are some other organizations that are working towards poverty alleviation in your community? Ask your friends, co-workers, and Bible study to get more ideas.
3. Reach out to these ministries and organizations to learn about their needs and ways volunteers can be involved. Consider the overall mission of the organization, what your role could be, time commitments, etc.

Discuss

1. Do these ministries' and organizations' efforts address the flourishing principles?
2. If yes, are there ways your gifts and talents can be used that fit with the available volunteer opportunities?
3. If no, are there ways the efforts can be adjusted to meet the principles?

Write

Describe any possible ministries and organizations that address the flourishing principles and how you could be involved in the effective work that they do.

Resources

- Guidestar offers a list of nonprofits in the United States—Use the advanced search to find nonprofits in your area that fit the criteria you are looking for: www.guidestar.org
- PovertyCure's global network: http://www.povertycure.org/globalnetwork/

STEP 4: What are you going to do?

Finally, let's put everything together. In this section, you will be able to put all the pieces together. You can assess all the options available to you, and decide how you want to serve!

Pray

Ask the Lord to be with you as you venture out into your community to work for its flourishing. Pray that he will guide you and make your efforts fruitful. Pray that God will use you to further his kingdom and that he will bring you into meaningful relationships with your poor neighbors.

Reflect

1. Put together the summaries of steps 1-3. You now have a description of the poverty landscape of your community, your comparative advantage in fighting poverty, and a list of possible opportunities to come alongside the poor.
2. Where is there overlap? Which of the opportunities you came up with in step 3 utilize your comparative advantage to serve a specific need in your community?
3. Are there needs in the community that are not being met by current organizations?

Discuss

1. Talk about the opportunities that are available to you and encourage one another to go out and work to promote flourishing.
2. If applicable, discuss the idea that there are needs in the community that are going unmet. Can you or your group meet these unmet needs in a way that is consistent with the flourishing principles?

Do

Choose an available opportunity with a current ministry or organization or make your own opportunity that meets unmet needs in the community. Whatever you do, make sure it respects the dignity of the poor and encourages them to take ownership of their development.

Share

Tweet us at @FaithWorkEcon to share what you've decided to do to serve your community and let us know about ministries and organizations that are working to advance flourishing!

CONCLUDING THOUGHTS

Recently, I sat down with Tony Casson, founder of Mission Muffins, a ministry of a DC men's homeless shelter called the Central Union Mission. Mission Muffins strives to serve men in the shelter by employing them in a bakery, teaching them marketable skills, and helping them find a full-time job after the program. At the time of our conversation, Mission Muffins had opened just two months prior. Tony said to me, "We have two (employees), who have redefined a lot of things for me. They've made me realize…the challenges facing them are a lot greater than I ever anticipated… So, it's a challenge. Probably not going to be the 6-month program that I anticipated it would be. But I do see that they take enormous pleasure in doing something they've never done before and doing something they never thought they could do. They make muffins."

During that conversation, Tony gave me insight into the difficulties people face as they strive to help the poor flourish. He was open and honest about the complications that were present in the program, but also communicated his patience, grace, and love for those he's serving. It is evident that he is in deep relationship with his employees and has made, and continues to make, adjustments to the program per their needs. He told me that one of the employees loved basketball, so he taught him baking skills in the way that a basketball coach would train his player. He highlighted some of his employees' best strengths, and shared what he had learned from his relationship with them. Though it is not easy, his comments also showed the impact it has already made—they are proud of baking muffins.

Talking with Tony reminded me that the task of loving our neighbors through service to the poor is tough to do, especially in the way that we have discussed it in this booklet. It is hard to form relationships. It is hard to develop gifts and talents. It is hard to push for sustainable change. It is also hard to hear that many of us have tried tactics that we now realize may have been more hurtful than helpful.

When I read Corbett and Fikkert's *When Helping Hurts* for the first time, I was certainly convicted of hurting those I was trying to help. This is tough news to swallow, and it can be discouraging. But, we cannot stop at discouragement. We are called to serve the poor and to do that, we must do the sometimes messy work of being in relationship with those we are serving. Let's be encouraged by the ways we've seen organizations described in this booklet at work in this way as well as motivated to continue our own efforts to effect flourishing.

This said, in the process of striving for sustainable and effective poverty-fighting, we cannot let perfect be the enemy of good. In difficult situations in which we are not sure what to do, we should lean toward mercy and grace. Steve Corbett and Brain Fikkert in *Helping Without Hurting in Church Benevolence* write,

> In those moments when you have done your best to understand the situation and you still simply do not know what to do, our counsel is to err on the side of giving rather than withholding material assistance. And as much as possible, do this in the context of a long-term empowering relationship that seeks to restore the individual or family to God's design for them as image-bearers.[62]

We *should* do our best to be effective as we serve the poor, but we cannot get so caught up that we lose sight of the goal—to love our neighbors. In the end, we are striving to improve how we work with the poor. We do not want these ideas to cause people to pull away from fighting poverty. We want our poverty efforts to double; we want people to get in the thick of it, to walk alongside the poor, and display the love of Christ. In Romans 13:8-10, the passage we discussed in Chapter 2, we were reminded that love is to do no harm. The type of love Paul is referring to is agape love. This love is the ultimate form of love as described in the Bible, and its qualifying characteristic is self-sacrifice.[63] To truly love the poor, it will take time and effort, and it will not be easy.

Finally, my hope is that you are inspired to do what you can to serve the poor in your community. As we have learned, macro-level changes are sometimes needed to make big changes in our communities; however, we cannot wait until these changes occur. We must go out, love our neighbors, and enact the change we can. Fighting poverty at the personal level, in relationship, is the most effective way to tackle the big problems we see around us, even if it seems like it isn't enough. With hundreds of thousands of people serving the poor on an individual level, respecting the poor, and allowing them to have ownership in their own development we can bring about dramatic changes in macro-level issues by working on the individual level. I challenge you to go out and be part of this change!

We will probably not see the end of poverty in our lifetime. But, God is sovereign and all-powerful, and his kingdom will be perfect—without blemish, without poverty, without hunger, without injustice. As we seek to serve our communities and love our neighbors, we must always keep this in mind and rely on Christ to do the work that we are unable to do ourselves. ■

BIBLIOGRAPHY

Rethinking How to Fight Poverty

- Bradley, Anne, and Art Lindsley, eds. *For the Least of These: A Biblical Answer to Poverty*. Grand Rapids: Zondervan, 2014.

- Corbett, Steve, and Brian Fikkert. *When Helping Hurts: How to Alleviate Poverty Without Hurting the Poor and Yourself*. Chicago: Moody Publishers, 2009.

- Coyne, Christopher. *Doing Bad by Doing Good: Why Humanitarian Action Fails*. Stanford, CA: Stanford University Press, 2013.

- Greer, Peter. *The Spiritual Danger of Doing Good*. Bloomington, MN: Bethany House Publishers, 2014.

- Lupton, Robert. *Toxic Charity: How Churches and Charities Hurt Those They Help, and How to Reverse It*. New York: HarperOne, 2012.

- PovertyCure, *PovertyCure*. DVD set. Directed by Michael Matheson Miller. 2012; Grand Rapids, MI: Acton Media. Documentary.

- PovertyCure, *Poverty, Inc.* DVD. Directed by Michael Matheson Miller. 2014; Grand Rapids, MI: Acton Media. Documentary.

International Poverty

- Acemo lu, Daron, and James A. Robinson. *Why Nations Fail: The Origins of Power, Prosperity, and Poverty*. New York: Crown Business, 2013.

- Easterly, William. *The Tyranny of Experts: Economists, Dictators, and the Forgotten Rights of the Poor*. New York: Basic Books, 2014.

- Easterly, William. *The White Man's Burden: Why the West's Efforts to Aid the Rest Have Done So Much Ill and So Little Good*. New York: Penguin, 2007.

- Grudem, Wayne, and Barry Asmus. *The Poverty of Nations: A Sustainable Solution*. Wheaton, IL: Crossway, 2013.

- Moyo, Dambisa. *Dead Aid: Why Aid is Not Working and How There is a Better Way for Africa*. New York: Farrar, Straus and Giroux, 2010.

Church-Centered Poverty Alleviation

- Corbett, Steve, and Brian Fikkert. *Helping Without Hurting in Church Benevolence: A Practical Guide to Walking with Low-Income People*. Chicago: Moody Publishers, 2015.

- Fekkert, Brian, and Russell Mask. *From Dependence to Dignity: How to Alleviate Poverty through Church-Centered Microfinance*. Grand Rapids: Zondervan, 2015.

- McConnell, Mez, and Mike McKinley. *Church in Hard Places: How the Local Church Brings Life to the Poor and Needy*. Wheaton, IL: Crossway, 2016.

Faith and Work Books

- Whelchel, Hugh. *All Things New: Rediscovering the Four-Chapter Gospel*. McLean, VA: The Institute for Faith, Work & Economics, 2016.

- Whelchel, Hugh. *How Then Should We Work? Rediscovering the Biblical Doctrine of Work*. Bloomington, IN: Westbow Press, 2012.

ENDNOTES

1. "Charitable Giving in America: Some Facts and Figures," National Center for Charitable Statistics, accessed March 25, 2016, http://nccs.urban.org/nccs/statistics/charitable-giving-in-america-some-facts-and-figures.cfm.

2. "Volunteering and Civic Life in America 2015," Corporation for National & Community Service, accessed March 25, 2016, https://www.volunteeringinamerica.gov/.

3. Carmen DeNavas-Walt, Bernadette D. Proctor, and U.S. Census Bureau "Income and Poverty in the United States: 2014," (Washington, DC: U.S. Government Printing Office, 2015), 13, https://www.census.gov/content/dam/Census/library/publications/2015/demo/p60-252.pdf.

4. Ibid.

5. Robert D. Lupton, *Toxic Charity: How Churches and Charities Hurt Those They Help* (And How to Reverse It) (New York: HarperCollins Publishers, 2011), 3-4.

6. Steve Corbett and Brian Fikkert, *When Helping Hurts: How to Alleviate Poverty Without Hurting the Poor and Yourself* (Chicago: Moody Publishers, 2009), 71.

7. Timothy C. Morgan, "Purpose Driven in Rwanda," *Christianity Today*, September 23, 2005, accessed October 28, 2016, http://www.christianitytoday.com/ct/2005/october/17.32.html.

8. Jonathan Pennington, "A Biblical Theology of Human Flourishing," The Institute for Faith, Work, and Economics, March 4, 2015, 14 https://tifwe.org/resource/a-biblical-theology-of-human-flourishing-2/.

9. Vaughan Roberts, *God's Big Picture: Tracing the Storyline of the Bible* (Downers Grove: InterVarsity Press, 2002), 22.

10. Pennington, "A Biblical Theology of Human Flourishing," 16.

11. Ibid, 17.

12. Jonathan Pennington, "'Sell Your Possessions and Give to The Poor': A Theological Reflection on Jesus' Teaching Regarding Personal Wealth and Charity," The Institute for Faith, Work, and Economics, July 9, 2015, accessed October 28, 2016, https://tifwe.org/resource/sell-your-possessions-and-give-to-the-poor-a-theological-reflection-on-jesus-teaching-regarding-personal-wealth-and-charity/.

13. Don Dunavant, "Man ~ Made in the Image of God," *SBC Life Journal of the Southern Baptist Convention*, October 2009, accessed October 28, 2016, http://www.sbclife.net/Articles/2009/10/sla6.

14. Glenn Sunshine, "The Image of God and Human Dignity," *The Christian Worldview Journal*, May 24, 2010, accessed October 28, 2016, http://www.colsoncenter.org/the-center/columns/call-response/15270-the-image-of-god-and-human-dignity.

15. J. I. Packer, "Reflected Glory," *Christianity Today*, December 1, 2003, accessed October 28, 2016, http://www.christianitytoday.com/ct/2003/december/20.56.html.

16. Oxford Dictionary, accessed April 1, 2016, http://www.oxforddictionaries.com/us/definition/american_english/dignity.

17. Philippians 2:8

18. Hugh Whelchel, *All Things New: Rediscovering the Four-Chapter Gospel* (McLean, VA. Institute for Faith, Work & Economics, 2016), 20.

19. Ibid, 35.

20. Steve Corbett and Brian Fikkert, *When Helping Hurts*, 81.

21. Tim Keller, *Jesus the King: Understanding the Life and Death of the Son of God* (New York: Penguin, 2011), 7.

22. Ibid, 9.

23. For more information about incommunicable vs. communicable attributes, please see Wayne A. Grudem, "The Character of God: 'Communicable Attributes,'" *Systematic Theology* (Grand Rapids: Zondervan, 1994): 185-225.

24. Peter Greer, "'Stop Helping Us:' A Call to Compassionately Move beyond Charity," in *For the Least of These: A Biblical Answer to Poverty*, eds. Anne Bradley and Art Lindsley (Grand Rapids: Zondervan, 2014), 232-233.

25. Ibid.

26. Ibid.

27. Ibid.

28 Ibid., 65.

29 Lupton, *Toxic Charity*, 3.

30 Spickard, "Six Words to a Pathway out of Oppression," *Jobs for Life*, September 10, 2013, accessed October 28, 2016, http://www.jobsforlife.org/blog/detail/view/66/six-words-to-a-pathway-out-of-oppression.

31 Anne McAdams, "Special Report: Wilmington Human Trafficking Survivor," WECT News 6, August 26, 2013, http://www.wect.com/story/23260417/special-report-human-trafficking-survivor-speaks.

32 Spickard, "Six Words."

33 Ibid.

34 "Frequently Asked Questions," Jobs for Life, accessed April 8, 2016, http://www.jobsforlife.org/frequently-asked-questions.

35 DeNavas-Walt and Proctor, "Income and Poverty," 16.

36 David Bass, *Clearing Obstacles to Work: A Wise Giver's Guide to Fostering Self-Reliance* (Washington, DC: The Philanthropy Roundtable, 2015), 16.

37 Steven Raphael and Rudolf Winter-Ebmer, "Identifying the Effect of Unemployment on Crime," *The Journal of Law & Economics* 44, no. 1 (April 2001): 259-283.

38 Edwin Slipek, Jr., "The Lost Neighborhood," *Style Weekly*, November 8, 2006, accessed October 28, 2016, http://www.styleweekly.com/richmond/the-lost-neighborhood/Content?oid=1363378.

39 Ibid.

40 Ibid.

41 Ibid.

42 "Our Mission," Strategies to Elevate People (STEP), accessed April 8, 2016, http://steprichmond.org/our-mission/.

43 Ibid.

44 "Programs," STEP, accessed April 8, 2016, http://steprichmond.org/programs/.

45 "Media," STEP, accessed April 8, 2016, http://steprichmond.org/news/media/.

46 "Home," STEP, accessed April 8, 2016, http://steprichmond.org.

47 Mary Bruce and John Bidgeland, *The Mentoring Effect: Young People's Perspectives on the Outcomes and Availability of Mentoring.* (Washington, DC: Civic Enterprises with Hart Research Associates for MENTOR: The National Mentoring Partnership, 2014), 3.

48 Ibid.

49 Ibid.

50 Brian A. Jacob and Jens Ludwig, "Improving educational outcomes for poor children," in *Changing Poverty, Changing Policies*, eds. Maria Cancian and Sheldon Danziger (New York: Russell Sage Foundation Press, 2009): 266-300.

51 Julie A. Phillips, "White, Black, and Latino Homicide Rates: Why the Difference?," Social Problems 49, no. 3 (2002): 349-373. Ordering: http://www.jstor.org/stable/10.1525/sp.2002.49.3.349.

52 Lupton, Toxic, 32-33.

53 "About Us," Tearfund, accessed April 8, 2016, http://www.tearfund.org/en/about_us/.

54 Ibid.

55 "Meseret," TearFund, accessed April 8, 2016, http://www.tearfund.org/en/give/give_main/shg/meseret/.

56 Ibid.

57 Ibid.

58 Greer, "'Stop Helping Us,'" 239.

59 Lupton, *Toxic Charity*, 20.

60 Corbett and Fikkert, *When Helping Hurts*, 134-135.

61 For a slightly different, but free, version of the Myers-Briggs Assessment, check out 16 Personalities: https://www.16personalities.com/.

62 Steve Corbett and Brian Fikkert with Katie Casselberry, *Helping Without Hurting in Church Benevolence* (Chicago: Moody Publishers, 2015), 11.

63 Jack Wellman, "What is Agape Love? A Bible Study," *Patheos*, May 2, 2014, accessed October 28, 2016. http://www.patheos.com/blogs/christiancrier/2014/05/02/what-is-agape-love-a-bible-study/.

ABOUT THE AUTHOR

Kathryn Feliciano is the ministry coordinator at Restoration Church in Washington, DC, where she leads the women's and children's ministries and handles various administrative responsibilities. She previously served as the manager of academic initiatives for the Institute for Faith, Work & Economics. She earned her master of arts in economics at George Washington University and has a bachelor of arts in economics from Christopher Newport University. She lives with her husband, Hector, in Washington, DC and enjoys serving the community through her church and various nonprofits. She also loves ice cream, summertime, and exploring the District.

ABOUT THE INSTITUTE
FOR FAITH, WORK & ECONOMICS

The Institute for Faith, Work & Economics™ (IFWE) is a non-profit, 501(c)(3) Christian research organization committed to promoting biblical and economic principles that help individuals find fulfillment in their work and contribute to a free and flourishing society.

IFWE's research starts with the belief that the Bible, as the inerrant Word of God, provides the authoritative and intellectual foundation for a proper understanding of work and economic truths that, when properly followed, can help individuals, companies, communities, and nations flourish.

IFWE's research is based on three core principles:

- Each person is created in God's image and, like him, has a desire to be creative and to find **fulfillment** using their God-given talents through work.
- All work, whether paid or volunteer, matters to God, and we as Christians are called to pursue excellence throughout the week—not just on Sundays—stewarding all that we've been given for God's glory and for the **flourishing** of society.
- Therefore, we as citizens must promote an economic environment that not only provides us the **freedom** to pursue our callings and flourish in our work but also reflects the inherent dignity of every human being.

Our desire is to help Christians view their work within the bigger picture of what God is doing in the world. Not only do we help Christians find personal fulfillment, but we also help them understand how to better alleviate poverty, address greed, and view possessions properly. With a biblical view of work and economics, we can partner together to be meaningful participants in God's plan to restore the world to the way he intended it to be.

START HERE

The Institute for Faith, Work & Economics provides many resources to help you live a life of freedom, fulfillment, and flourishing. These tools are designed to fit into your life and provide biblical encouragement and guidance to your walk with God.

BLOG
Get our daily or weekly blog updates in your inbox.
BLOG.TIFWE.ORG

RESEARCH
Download free in-depth studies to further your understanding of faith, work, and economics.
RESEARCH.TIFWE.ORG

SOCIALIZE
Connect with IFWE on social media and join the conversation.
FACEBOOK.COM / FAITHWORKECON
TWITTER.COM / FAITHWORKECON

BOOK STORE

Get our latest releases and educational products.

STORE.TIFWE.ORG

DONATE

Become a partner in bringing about flourishing.

DONATE.TIFWE.ORG

PARTICIPATE

Find information about student groups, upcoming events, and other opportunities to get involved.

CONNECT.TIFWE.ORG

INSTITUTE FOR
FAITH, WORK
& ECONOMICS

INSTITUTE FOR
FAITH, WORK
& ECONOMICS